SAINT JC
MARY VIANNEY
THE CURÉ D'ARS

CTS Children's Books

Contents

Text by Silvia Vecchini
Illustrations by Giusy Capizzi
Translated by Pierpaolo Finaldi

Saint John Mary Vianney - The Curé D'Ars: Published 2010 by the Incorporated Catholic Truth Society, 40-46 Harleyford Road,London SE11 5AY. Tel: 020 7640 0042; Fax: 020 7640 0046; www.cts-online.org.uk. Copyright © 2010 The Incorporated Catholic Truth Society in this English-language edition.

ISBN: 978 1 86082 676 4   CTS Code CH 28

Translated from the original Italian Edition: **San Giovanni Maria Vianney - Il Curato D'Ars** - ISBN 978-88-6124-163-3, published by Il Pozzo di Giacobbe, Corso Vittorio Emanuele 32/34, 91100 Trapani (TP), Italy © 2010 Crispino di Girolamo.

A VILLAGE PARISH

In 1817 the tiny village of Ars in France was unknown to everyone except its 300 poor inhabitants. When Fr John Mary Vianney arrived in his new parish he found that no one was very interested in God. Few people went to Sunday Mass and for most people, the only time they thought about God was when they made a quick examination of conscience before going to bed at night.

ALL ABOARD FOR THE VILLAGE OF ARS!

In just a few years, the little village of Ars had become very important for the Christian life of all the nearby parishes and towns, and then for all of France. Soon Ars had become famous all over Europe and great crowds came from far and wide to visit the village.

From 1830 until 1845 the number of people who wanted to visit Ars was so great that a special ticket office was opened at Lyon train station which only sold tickets for Ars.

The ticket to Ars was different from other tickets. It was valid for eight days so that everyone who went had enough time to meet the parish priest and talk to him.

What was it that had suddenly transformed a tiny village into such an important place? Why were so many people travelling to Ars? Who was the parish priest that everyone wanted to see? Let's step back in time and find out...

A SIMPLE CHILDHOOD

John Mary Vianney was born on 8th May 1786 to a family of farmers in Dardilly near Lyon in France. John was the fourth of seven children. His family all prayed together and took special care of the poor people who lived nearby.

In 1789, when John was just three years old, the French revolution began.

Very soon the whole of France was affected by the revolution and there was a lot of fear and violence. Many laws were made that discriminated against Christians. Churches were closed and many priests were forced to stop being priests.
John's family carried on going to Mass in secret. The priests who said the secret Masses had all refused to give up their mission and had remained faithful to Rome and to the Pope.

John was a good boy and grew up helping his parents look after sheep on the farm. His favourite game was a sort of hoop-la played with wooden rings. He wasn't very clever or well-educated but he was a brave boy. Some of the priests who had refused to become priests of the revolution were secretly looked after on John's parents' farm. It was thanks to one of these priests who was hiding in a barn on the farm that John made his First Confession when he was 11 years old. He had to wait another two years before making his First Holy Communion in secret with another priest who was hiding on the farm.

The courageous example of those priests who had risked their lives to give John the Sacraments of Reconciliation and the Eucharist made a deep impression on him. He knew that it was thanks to them that he had met God and the desire to be just like them began to grow in his heart.

A PATIENT TEACHER

When John was sure that he wanted to become a priest, he told his family.

His father Matthew could not spare him from the farm, there was too much work to do and not enough money to pay for his studies at the seminary, so he had to wait.

When he was twenty years old John was finally able to move to a village nearby called Ecully where Fr Balley the parish priest had a small school. John had only learnt to read and write at the age of seventeen and had only gone to the village school long enough to learn the basics. He soon found it very difficult at Fr Balley's school.

For three years he studied French and Latin but his grades were poor because he was a slow learner and had a bad memory. He often got discouraged but Fr Balley helped him and encouraged him to carry on.

In the meantime John was called up to join the army. He didn't want to go and became a deserter which meant he had to stay hidden for a time. After many adventures he was able to go back home. He started his studies again with great difficulty and in 1815 was able to go to the seminary in Lyon. His first exam was a disaster and the fact that all the lessons were in Latin made things even more difficult.

John went back to Fr Balley who once again helped him and encouraged him not to give up the studies he needed to complete in order to become a priest.

The parish priest of Ecully turned out to be a patient teacher and a sincere friend. He continued to help John until he passed all the exams necessary to become a priest.

FATHER JOHN

Finally after two years John was ready to become a priest. Everyone could see that even though he found studying difficult, he had made great progress. It was clear that he was a good, simple man whose vocation was sincere.

The vicar general was sure that John had the makings of a good priest and that 'God would do the rest'.

At the age of 29, John was ordained on 12th August 1815. He was appointed as curate to help Fr Balley.

John began his life as a priest with his teacher and spiritual guide in Ecully. He lived an austere life and soon began to dedicate himself with great care and in a special way to the Sacrament of Reconciliation.

Two years later, Fr Balley died and Fr John was left by himself. A new parish was chosen for Fr John among simple people in the country, it seemed just right for a priest who was not that clever. John was sent to Ars en Dombes to become the new parish priest of the village.

THE LITTLE FLOCK

John was sure that the village of Ars had been entrusted to him by God to look after, like a little flock of sheep.

And like the good shepherd described by Jesus in the Gospels, John didn't want to forget anyone, he wanted to reach everyone, especially the lost sheep.

For this reason it was not enough for John to speak to the few people who turned up in his church. He wanted to reach all the inhabitants of Ars and to renew the heart of that little village.

He decided that it was important to give a good example, so he lived a life of prayer and penitence and always put God first.
He began to visit all the families in Ars, one by one, and spoke with all of them personally. He spent time with each family as though they were the most important people in the village.

Fr John started teaching catechism to children and opened a school which he called 'La Providence'. It soon became a place where orphans and abandoned children were brought to be looked after and no child was ever turned away.

A QUIET LITTLE VOICE

Fr John invited everyone to mass on Sunday and tried to abolish any kind of work on the day that should be dedicated to rest and to God. He asked his parishioners not to drink too much and to live a simple life.

Beginning with these little things, John began to guide his parish with increasing energy.

But he concentrated especially on two things: his Sunday sermons and on hearing confessions.

The number of people who came to see him slowly increased, not only the inhabitants of Ars who used to stay away from church, but also people from nearby towns who had heard about the young priest. His fame soon spread from city to city and more and more people travelled to Ars to meet him.

Reports from the time say that he had a quiet, little voice and that because of all the crowds who came to listen to him it was hard to hear anything… but for many it was enough to hear just a few words and their lives were changed.

A READER OF HEARTS

The people who came to Ars wanted to do more than just listen to him in church, they wanted to speak with him personally and go to him for confession. Fr John had already begun spending many hours every day in the confessional so that everyone could come and have their sins forgiven. He knew that in the Sacrament of Reconciliation everybody can speak freely and open their hearts to God and return to him who is full of forgiveness. Jesus said to his disciples: "those whose sins you forgive, they are forgiven" and John wanted to do what Jesus said. For this reason he was always ready to welcome whoever came to him to ask God for forgiveness: with each day that passed he was better able to read people's hearts, their doubts and their sufferings.

Every sort of person went to Fr John including the rich and poor, educated and uneducated, monks and nuns and ordinary Catholics, even bishops and priests, and John was able to give precious advice to all of them.

He always told people to pray the Angelus or the Rosary so that they would stay close to God and to the prayer of the Church.

He once said: "Private prayer is like straw scattered here and there: If you set it on fire it makes a lot of little flames. But gather these straws into a bundle and light them, and you get a mighty fire, rising like a column into the sky; public prayer is like that."

NOTHING IS IMPOSSIBLE!

So many people gathered around Fr John that in the last years of his life, he wasn't able to take a few steps outside his house without having crowds following him and asking him to bless them or to say a few words.

Sometimes Fr John thought that he was not worthy of the mission that he had been given and that it would be best if he escaped to live in a monastery on his own, but everyone begged him to stay and continue his work among the people.

How did Fr John manage to touch the heart of so many people? It was certainly not because he was clever, nor because of his human qualities or the effort that he put into listening to people. John had a gift, he was able to communicate to others what he felt so deeply himself: the friendship of Jesus.

Fr John's way of bringing people back to God was simple: he loved Jesus deeply and for this reason the people who gathered around him believed what he said. John loved the words of Jesus and his saving message, he loved the Sacrament of the Eucharist where Jesus becomes present for us all and he loved praying because it brings us close to God.

Towards the end of his life, although he was old, more than a thousand pilgrims came to meet him every week. The little village of Ars had really changed just like Fr John wanted, and not just Ars but many towns nearby.

Fr John had spent his whole life giving himself to Jesus as a priest and God had had kept his promise that he would do great things through John, because as the Gospel says: "nothing is impossible for God!"

PATRON SAINT
OF PARISH PRIESTS

Fr John spent 41 years in Ars and died on 4th August in 1859. In 1925 he was declared a saint by Pius XI and a few years later in 1929, the same Pope made him the Patron Saint of Parish Priests.

John Mary Vianney became a saint not because he had any extraordinary talents, but because he lived his mission with faith and humility. He searched for God and helped others to search for him. He made every moment of his life holy and helped those around him to become holy too.

In 2009 Pope Benedict XVI on the 150th anniversary of the death of John Mary Vianney who loved his ministry as a priest with all his heart, declared a year for priests: a special time for every priest to rediscover his true mission.

SOME THOUGHTS OF THE CURÉ D'ARS

"In a soul that is united with God, it is always springtime."

"This is the glorious duty of man: to pray and to love. If you pray and love, that is where your happiness lies."

"The saints knew themselves better than they knew others: that is why they were humble."

"When we pray properly, sorrows disappear like snow before the sun."

"A pure soul is with God like a child is with its mother: the child kisses and strokes the mother and she kisses and strokes the child."

"Humility is like a balance: the lower one side goes, the higher it rises on the other."

22

JOHN MARY VIANNEY

A PRAYER

Lord, we pray for all priests,
that they may remember
the tenderness of your calling
and never lose the hope
with which they began to follow you.
May they search for you in prayer,
and may their hearts be close to your heart;
so that they may always be able to
give words of friendship, comfort,
and truth to everyone they meet.
May they know how to guide people towards you
and to accompany them on that path night and day.
May they see you in the poor and the suffering
and teach others to do the same.
May they bravely proclaim your kingdom
and remind the whole world of your love.

Amen